Hemisferio Cuir

*An Anthology of Young Queer
Latin American Poetry*

Selected and translated by
LEO BOIX
2025

First published in 2025 by Fourteen Publishing.
fourteenpoems.com

Design and typeset by Stromberg Design.
strombergdesign.co.uk

Proofreading and copy editing by Lara Kavanagh.
lk-copy.com

Printed by P2D Ltd, Westoning, Bedfordshire, UK.

The poets published in this book have asserted their right to be identified as the authors of this work in accordance with the Copyright, Designs and Patents Act 1988.

This book is sold subject to the conditions that it shall not be lent, resold, hired out or otherwise circulated without the publisher's prior consent. Any republishing of the individual works must be agreed in advance.

ISBN: 978-1-7384871-5-8

Here is my face
I speak for my difference.

Pedro Lemebel

CONTENTS

ARGENTINA
Washington Atencio 14
Paula Galíndez 22
Silvina Giaganti 28
Pablo Romero 32

BOLIVIA
César Antezana/Flavia Lima 42

CHILE
Gabriela Contreras 50
Pablo Jofré 54

COLOMBIA
Flor Bárcenas Feria 62
Ana López Hurtado 66

COSTA RICA
Ronald Campos López 74
David Ulloa 82

CUBA
Yordán Rey Oliva 92

DOMINICAN REPUBLIC
Ju Puello 98

ECUADOR
Tibiezas Dager 104
Victoria Vaccaro García 110

EL SALVADOR
Alberto López Serrano 120

GUATEMALA
Manuel Gabriel Tzoc Bucup 126

HONDURAS
Yasón Serra 134
V. Andino Díaz 140

MEXICO
Ingrid Bringas 148
César Cañedo 156
Daniel Nizcub 160

NICARAGUA
Magaly Castillo 168

PARAGUAY
Edu Barreto 174

PERU
Fiorella Terrazas 180

PUERTO RICO
Myr Olivares 186
Alejandra Rosa Morales 194

URUGUAY
Ivix Pereira 204

VENEZUELA
Enza García Arreaza 212

INTRODUCTION

What is the place of queerness in the Latin American poetry of the 21st century? Is there a way to define a heterogeneous collective that transcends national boundaries, cultural specificities, and gender identities?

Solidarity, resistance, LGBTQIA+ affectivity, queer love, and transgression are just some of the strongest currents in the river of young Latin American verse. A presence that is often evoked through what Brad Epps calls 'the tension between being and coming (...), fragmentation and wholeness, recuperation and reinvention, reality and representation.'[1]

In 2020, while writing a detailed report on contemporary Latin American poetry for the Poetry Translation Centre (PTC) in London, I was inspired to translate the work of Argentine poet Diana Bellessi, a pioneer in feminist, LGBTQIA+, and lesbian poetry in Argentina. This experience made me realise the importance of creating an anthology of young queer Latin American poets, which would be the first of its kind in the UK and much of the English-speaking world.

Thanks to the editor of *fourteen poems*, Ben Townley-Canning, who believed in this project from the start, and the generosity of so many queer poets, editors, translators, and colleagues from Latin America and beyond, we now have *Hemisferio Cuir*.

The anthology explores the Latin American region and its cultural diaspora as a liberating territory for political action and dissent related to transgressive sexualities, queer desires, and body conceptions. This anthology features LGBTQIA+ voices from various Spanish-speaking countries, translated into English, and delves into what it means to be a young queer Latin American poet.

The poets in this anthology come from countries across Latin America: Argentina, Bolivia, Chile, Colombia, Costa Rica, Cuba, Dominican Republic, Ecuador, El Salvador, Guatemala, Honduras, Mexico, Nicaragua, Paraguay, Peru, Puerto Rico, Uruguay, and Venezuela. The collection addresses recurring themes such as family relationships, the queer body, discrimination and trans sensibilities, as well as love, loss, and sexual desire, in a post-patriarchal society.

This literary journey begins with Argentinian Washington Atencio's voluptuous poem "Our Shadow Flows Into the River", where bodies, landscape, and queer desires collide. It is followed by his compatriot Paula Galíndez's ode to the complexities of a mother-daughter relationship in "But if I'm honest", and Silvina Giaganti's "She Said That Love I Had," where the figure of a mother and a psychologist form a specular version in which to project frustrations and a sense of loss. Also from Argentina is Pablo Romero, whose "SELFIE" explores the difficulties of a gay break-up.

Bolivian poet César Antezana/Flavia Lima's untitled poem shows us trans bodies that 'dream the abject and despair'. From Chile, Gabriela Contreras's "We are the barricade" sings to the power of politics and revolution among dissident women, and Pablo Jofre's "Ode to Querelle of Brest" evokes gay sensibilities via Jean Genet's famous antihero.

The Afro-Caribbean poet Flor Bárcenas Feria, from Colombia, dazzles us with "The Water of Dreams" and a poignant meditation on father-son/daughter relationships, while Ana López Hurtado, also from Colombia, deals with naming the body queer, as the poet writes: 'only I name myself:/charm that travels through the skin/tangle, trance, sheltered.'

From Costa Rica, both Ronald Campos López and David Ulloa explore gay love, desire, and pleasure in wondrous poems of luminous beauty, while from Cuba, Yordán Rey Oliva evokes his island of homosexual desires, where he 'learned the magic/of waiting' for his lover. The Afro-Dominican transmasculine writer Ju Puello writes a Whitmanian ode to himself, celebrating his race, identity, and post-colonial history in a scintillating poem titled "I Afro-Love Myself".

From Ecuador, the trans poets Tibiezas Dager and Victoria Vaccaro García shed light on what it means to write, love, and exist as a trans person in a dangerous and unequal world. Salvadorian poet Alberto López Serrano writes a delicate song about the pleasures of one's own body in his work "THE SAILING BOAT II" merging the self with the river: 'I love you, my body; you enchant me, and the river is my accomplice in this secret.' In his powerful poem "FECALITY IN OBLIVION", Guatemalan Mayan K'iche' poet Manuel Gabriel Tzoc Bucup intertwines the abject and earthy with the object of desire. Meanwhile, Honduran poet Yasón Serra's "Lamb" evokes the religious and the spiritual tinged with homoerotic desires. Also from Honduras is V. Andino Díaz, whose work "Female Poets in Love" takes the reader on a journey to Tegucigalpa, delving into its social inequalities and dangerous 'lonely streets'.

Mexican poets Ingrid Bringas, César Cañedo, and Daniel Nizcub all explore queerness, the queer body, loss, and gender identity from many different perspectives and sensibilities, including the trans, gay, and lesbian points of view. In contrast,

Nicaragua poet Magaly Castillo's "How to Be Happy Living in Nicaragua" mixes dark humour and irony in a poem of self-reflection that plays on music and rhythm.

Edu Barreto, from Paraguay, also uses humour in his poem "Maintenance and Repair", where he writes about maintenance men at work, gay desire, and a sense of being broken, while Peruvian Fiorella Terrazas offers a futuristic techno-digital-queer poem in their dazzling "The Number Meme".

Puerto Rican trans poet and translator Roque Raquel Salas Rivera has translated into English a series of poems by Myr Olivares, including the compelling "Cleanse", about family relationships, naming oneself as a trans person, and the political act of being proud. Also from Puerto Rico is Alejandra Rosa Morales, with their poem "[Post]humous Poem" on lesbian desire, Caribbean experiences, and breaking with a heteronormative family. Ivix Pereira, from Uruguay, also explores growing up as a lesbian girl with her Barbies making love 'like in the films'.

Finally, Venezuelan poet and short-story writer Enza García Arreaza weaves through a cinematic poem of rebellion, despair, and secrets as she writes: 'It's good to have a secret/to know that there's a planet in search of its name.'

In his influential work *Translating the Queer: Body Politics and Transnational Conversations*,[2] Héctor Domínguez Ruvalcaba explains that despite a historical hostility toward sexual difference in modern Latin American society, a queer politics has emerged in literature and the arts as a response to conservative intolerance. He suggests that queerness can be viewed as a disruptive aspect of modernity and as a way to de-patriarchalise the state and society.

I believe *Hemisferio Cuir: An Anthology of Young Queer Latin American Poetry* is an attempt in that direction and will provide readers with a glimpse of the political and poetic forces of change, resistance, and hope surging in Latin America.

Leo Boix, London, September 2024

---

1 Epps, Brad, "Virtual Sexuality", in *¿Entiendes?, ¿Entiendes? Queer Readings, Hispanic Writings*, edited by Emilie Bergmann and Paul Julian Smith, 323, Durham, NC: Duke University Press, 1995

2 Ruvalcaba, H.D., *Translating the Queer: Body Politics and Transnational Conversations*, Zed Books, London, 2016

ARGENTINA

WASHINGTON ATENCIO

Nuestra sombra volcada en el río

Abro bocas
rompo el aire con la lengua
lanzo todas las chispitas.

Él me mira
me contiene con los ojos.

Cruza el río
a lo lejos un caballo.
La llanura lo verdea.

En la tarde busco el cielo
lo acaricio
lo revuelco
me deshago.

Agua estalla en la laguna
otro mar nos da respiro
otro río me atraviesa.

ARGENTINA

Our Shadow Flows Into the River

I open mouths
tear the air with my tongue
throw all the sparks.

He looks at me
holds me with his eyes.

Crossing the river
in the distance a horse.
The llanura[3] greens it.

In the evening I search for the sky
caressing
wrestling
dissolving.

Water gushes into the lagoon
another sea gives us breath
another river goes through me.

This poem was translated by Jon Russell Herring with the
Poetry Translation Centre workshop led by Leo Boix.

3 In Argentina, a vast area of flat, often treeless, grass-covered land.

WASHINGTON ATENCIO

Terrario

Arreglás el jardín y te miro.

La naranja es un sol
a la siesta, relámpago cítrico
estallido en mi lengua.

Mis manos
vuelven al niño
que busca semillas,
porotos, granos de maíz.

Resultaba fácil
la tarea de naturales
viviendo tan cerca del suelo.

El campo fue mi germinador.

Bebimos la luz con fauces abiertas
nombramos el cielo y el agua,
quisimos brotar.

En tus manos
llenas de tierra
escupo una semilla
y espero.

ARGENTINA

Terrarium

You work in the garden and I look at you.

The orange is a sun
in the siesta, citrus lightning
burst on my tongue.

My hands
return to the child
in search of seeds,
beans, maize grains.

It was easy
to do the Science homework
living so close to the ground.

The countryside was my germinator.

We drank the light with open jaws
we named the sky and the water,
we wanted to sprout.

In your hands
full of earth
I spit a seed
and wait.

WASHINGTON ATENCIO

Ciclo

Dibujo enredaderas en tu cuello
y mi respiración abre
todas las flores. Palpito
la siesta de higueras y naranjos.
Acaricio hasta el rayo que se acuesta
en tu torso
perdido entre fardos.

Anido tu hombro
gorrión apenas.
Me disuelve el horizonte
la noche desgaja mi canto.

Olvido el hambre,
vuelvo a nacer en el trigo
que brota
cuando cerrás los ojos.

ARGENTINA

Cycle

I draw vines on your neck
and my breath opens
all the flowers. I pulsate
the siesta of fig and orange trees.
I caress even the lightning that lies down
on your torso
lost among bales.

I nest on your shoulder
almost sparrow.
The horizon dissolves me
the night tears my song apart.

I forget hunger,
I'm born again in the wheat
that sprouts
when you close your eyes.

WASHINGTON ATENCIO

WASHINGTON ATENCIO (b Entre Ríos, Argentina, 1986) lives in Paraná and teaches at the secondary, tertiary, and university levels. In 2019, he published *Una hoguera de jazmines* (Camalote) and was part of the collection *Tres Poemas* (Ediciones Arroyo). Some of his poems have received prizes and mentions. He manages the virtual bookshop Jacarandá (@jacaranda.libreria) and co-organises the poetry cycle Río Abajo. In February 2020 he published *Nuestra sombra volcada en el río* (Agua Viva).

ARGENTINA

PAULA GALÍNDEZ

Pero si soy sincera

pienso que la expiación debe ser
como cuando mamá metía las manos
entre llamas
y removía las tripas
de vaca.

Azul púrpura
plumas naranja
sus brazos ondeaban y ella
iba de lleno
al ojo de la luz.

Nunca entendí ese juego
de dejar que te acaricien el brazo
las lenguas del fuego, de acercar
la piel a lo que consume.
Debo tener algo
inherentemente frío adentro.

Pero lo de mamá
es más palpable,

algo en sus movimientos
se parece menos a la moraleja
y más a la historia.

But if I'm honest

I think atonement must be
like when mother used to stick her hands
in the flames
stirring the tripe
of a cow.

Purple blue
orange plumes
her arms waved and she
went straight
into the eye of the light.

I never understood that game
of letting your arm be touched by
tongues of fire, of bringing
the skin to what consumes it.
I must be
inherently cold inside.

But mother's way
is more palpable,

something in her movement
is less of a moral
and more of the story.

PAULA GALÍNDEZ

Una parra sube

por tu pierna,

el sol en la piel
deja su huella.

Es suave el olor
que sueltan las flores
abiertas al verano,

suave como la hoja
de malvón y madera
como el vino.

Es ahí, con la lengua
hundida en tu sabor
donde olvido esta tarde
todo el hambre.

ARGENTINA

A vine climbs

up your leg,

the sun on your skin
leaves its trace.

How soft the scent
that flowers release
when open to the summer,

soft as the leaf
of a malvón and woody
like wine.

It is there, with my tongue
sunk in your flavour
that I forget in the afternoon
all this hunger.

PAULA GALÍNDEZ

PAULA GALÍNDEZ (b Argentina, 1993) is a poet, translator, and translation professor born in Argentina. She earned a BA in Literary and Audiovisual Translation in English, and translated books from English and German into Spanish and Spanish into English. In 2021, she received a grant from the National Endowment for the Arts to edit and translate an anthology of 19th-century, English-speaking women poets, and she was selected for the Winter Writers Retreat at Banff Centre for Arts and Creativity to work on her new book, *28 Ways of Reading a Mother*. In 2022 she took part in the Poetry Translation Centre's Queer Digital Residency.

ARGENTINA

SILVINA GIAGANTI

Me dijo que amor tuve

A mi mamá le cuesta abrazarme
y preguntarme en qué ando.
Creo que no sabe qué estudié
ni de qué me recibí
pero me hace comida
para que traiga a casa
y hasta hace poco me ayudó
a pagar la obra social.
Ahora gano más
que las dos jubilaciones
juntas de mis padres
y me da una vergüenza enorme.
Mi psicóloga me dijo
que seguramente mi mamá
no hablaba mucho
conmigo ni con nadie
porque le pasaron cosas
que la metieron para adentro.
Y que si no me hubiera querido
ni me hubiera dado
los cuidados
que de bebé necesité
no hubiera sobrevivido.
Que amor tuve, eso me dijo.

ARGENTINA

She Said That Love I Had

My mother finds it hard to hug me
and ask me how I'm doing.
I think she doesn't know what I studied
nor what exams I passed
but she cooks me food
for me to take home
and until recently she helped me
to pay my social security.
Now I earn more
than the pensions of both my parents
put together
and it embarrasses me enormously.
My psychologist told me
that my mum probably
didn't talk much
with me or anybody else
because things happened to her
that made her turn inwards.
And that if she hadn't loved me
and hadn't taken care
of my needs as a baby
I wouldn't have survived.
That love I had, she said.

SILVINA GIAGANTI

SILVINA GIAGANTI (b Argentina, 1976) is a philosopher and writer. She published her first collection of poems, *Tarda en Apagarse,* in 2018. Her poems are autobiographical and tackle issues that Giaganti faces in her personal and professional life. She says her poems emerged from memory, from moments she couldn't forget that are connected to places in her life, streets, and neighbourhoods.

ARGENTINA

PABLO ROMERO

SELFIE

No borré (como vos) la foto que nos sacamos frente al espejo
sin saber si eran tus ojos los que me miraban o el reflejo de un otro
que nunca acabé de conocer.
Mi dolor no es lo hermoso de escribir la palabra tiempo sino lo atroz
de existir en contra: no borré (como vos) la imagen de mi cabeza
anclada a tu hombro para siempre, tus manos haciendo hueco
en mi cintura.
No borré (como vos) con rabia nuestra historia:
ya no hay pruebas de que estuvimos, de que fuimos en el otro
lo que llena la falta, el milagro de la fuerza que detiene
la catástrofe.
Nos encanta perder contra el deseo:
esto que escribo es la evidencia de haber sido.

SELFIE

I didn't delete (like you did) the photo we took of ourselves in front of the mirror
not knowing if it was your eyes looking back at me or the reflection of an other
that I never got to know.
My pain is not the beauty of writing the word 'time' but the atrociousness
of being against it: I didn't delete (like you) the image of my head
forever anchored to your shoulder, your hands making a hole
in my waist.
I didn't delete (like you) with rage our history:
there is no longer proof that we were, that we were in each other
what fills the absence, the miracle of the force that stops
the catastrophe.
We love to lose against desire:
this that I write is the evidence of having been.

PABLO ROMERO

DESLUGAR DE ENUNCIACIÓN

Escribo lo sucediendo: mi género
no es gramatical
:
yo   puede morir gramaticalmente
en mi poema
yo   puede desaparecer en la noche
de la noche.

Amé un hombre y su nombre ardió
en mi boca como un río: mar de piedras,
dientes que bruxan de deseo.

Escribo lo sucediendo: mi escritura
no tiene distancia   biográfica

cuando digo aquí en realidad digo aquí
:
cuando digo aquí   la palabra señala
como un dedo
(apunta) dispuesta a romper la distancia
entre la boca   y el silencio
:

yo   quiere olvidar   mi vida.

Soñé el amor imposible
entre la imagen   y la palabra
que mi cuerpo deseaba (por fin)
la idea de un cuerpo
y amaba el amor
con cada mano que tiende la furia

soñé
que fijaba mi poema a la lengua
del hombre que ardía en mi lengua
(como un río)

ARGENTINA

ENUNCIATION DISPLACEMENT

I write what is happening: my gender
is not grammatical
:
I   is capable of dying grammatically
in my poem
I   is capable of disappearing in the night
of the night

I loved a man and his name burned
in my mouth like a river: a sea of stones,
teeth clattering   of desire.

I write what (is) happening: my writing
lacks biographical   distance

when I say here I'm really saying here
:
when I say here   the word points
like a finger
(points) willingly to break the distance
between my mouth   and silence
:

I   wants to forget   my life.

I dreamt the impossible love
between the image and the word
my body desired (at last)
the idea of a body
and I loved the love
with every hand that tends the rage

I dreamt
that I fixed my poem to the tongue
of the man that burned in my tongue
(like a river)

PABLO ROMERO

para enseñarle al idioma
las palabras del desamparo.

Yo   puede morir entre nosotros
y en manos de mi texto

yo   quiere renunciar
a la sombra   de ser hombre
al asombro   de ser hambre

ARGENTINA

to teach language
the words of homelessness.

I is capable of dying among us
and at the hands of my text

I   wants to renounce
the shadow   of being a man
the wonder   of hunger

PABLO ROMERO

PABLO ROMERO (b Tucumán, Argentina, 1999) is a poet, editor, workshop leader, and translator. He is the author of *Los días de Babel* (Mexico, 2015), *Palabras tectónicas* (Argentina 2022, reed, Chile, 2022), and *La jaula del hambre* (Spain, 2024). He lived in Slovakia as a Rotary International exchange student and translates Slavic poetry. His translations include Milán Rufus, Milá Haugová, T.S. Eliot, Walt Whitman, and Katherine Mansfield. He was awarded the Premio Festival Poesía Ya! 2023 by the Centro Cultural Kirchner, the Premio a la Trayectoria de la Feria Itinerante del Libro (Tucumán), and has been a finalist for the Premio Loewe de Poesía Joven 2023 and the Premio Fundación Antonio Ródenas 2024. His work has been partially translated into French, Italian, and Portuguese. He is currently studying for a BA in Literature at the National University of Tucumán. Since 2019, he has co-directed the poetry publisher Aguacero Ediciones.

ARGENTINA

BOLIVIA

CÉSAR ANTEZANA/FLAVIA LIMA

Sin título

la humedad nos obliga a pernoctar a la intemperie de
nuestra caída

somos como un barranco después de los escombros y
las hemorroides

mis zapatos de tacón embarrados

debajo de tu cuerpo de paraguas

    exhausto

        salpicado de otro modo por el mismo rezo

            nuestros cuerpos en desahucio
            sueñan lo abyecto

                y desesperan

Untitled

Humidity compels us to spend the night outdoors in the open
of our fall

we're like a ravine after the rubble and
the haemorrhoids

my muddy high heels

beneath your umbrella body

    exhausted

        splattered in another way by the same prayer

            our bodies in eviction
            dream the abject

                and despair

CÉSAR ANTEZANA/FLAVIA LIMA

Intensidad

encuentro en mi cama

una serpiente en el momento exacto en que cambia de piel

      un hueso se atora en mi garganta y jadeo

luego lloro

luego muere

Intensity

I found in my bed

a serpent at the exact moment when it changes
its skin

        a bone gets stuck in my throat and I pant

then I cry

then it dies

CÉSAR ANTEZANA/FLAVIA LIMA

CÉSAR ANTEZANA/FLAVIA LIMA (b La Paz, Bolivia, 1979) is a poet who has been involved in the trans/cultural space ALMATROSTE (since 2004), the artisanal publishing house of the same name (since 2007), and the fanzine *La zurda siniestra*, co-organisers of the FLIA La Paz (independent and self-managed book fair). They have published the narrative book *Zzz...* and the poetry collections *El Muestrario de las pequeñas muertes* (Ed. Almatroste), *Cuerpos imperfectos,* and *Masochistics* (Yolanda Bedregal National Poetry Prize, 2017), among others. Their most recent book is *Cuerpos, Populacho y Escritura* (Editorial Matabuey, 2023), an anthology of their most recent work. César Antezana/Flavia Lima is a postgraduate student of literature at the UMSA in La Paz, a believer in anarchist praxis and vindicates "QUEER feminism in all its monstrosity".

ID
BOLIVIA

CHILE

GABRIELA CONTRERAS

Somos barricada

donde el fuego no es lengua voraz
más bien cenizas que nunca se rinden
se ven inofensivas
pero si te acercas arden

podemos morir en el pecho
pero estar brotando desde los muslos
debajo del caparazón
así ensamblamos el error de ser nosotras

nuestros cuerpos incorregibles
son revelaciones fracturadas
que perviven
inscribiendo subversiones entre labios
entre grasas inflamables

como tu mano dentro mío
la inevitable complicidad
entre temblor y palabra

nosotras
las geografías desobedientes
tuvimos que inventarnos un suelo
una hablada del derrumbe
formamos archipiélagos
conocimos el lenguaje de la ausencia
rotas
migramos más allá
del poderoso relato de la ganancia

tenemos la necesidad de incendiar
por todas las veces
que el ardor nos fue negado

We are the barricade

where fire is not a ravenous tongue
but rather ashes that never give up
they look harmless
but if you get closer, they burn

we can die in the chest
but we are surging from the thighs
under the shell
so we assemble the mistake of being us, women

our incorrigible bodies
are fractured revelations
that survive
inscribing subversions between lips
between flammable fats

like your hand inside me
the inevitable complicity
between tremor and words

we, women,
the disobedient geographies
we had to invent a place for ourselves
a discourse of collapse
we formed archipelagos
we knew the language of absence
broken
we migrated beyond
the powerful narrative of profit

we need to set fire
for all the times
that burning was denied to us

GABRIELA CONTRERAS

GABRIELA CONTRERAS (b Melipilla, Chile, 1983) is a writer who explores themes of bodily diversity, lesbofeminism, racism, and migration. She has authored several works, including *Leporina* (2012) and *Subterránea* (2014), both with Editorial Moda y Pueblo, and *Humedales* (FEA Editorial, 2017), the latter being published in Mexico. In 2022, she released *Caguama, escritos de una lesbiana gorda*, a piece that combines narrative and poetry to narrate the story of a lesbian woman's journey abroad in search of love. Along with the Mexican performer La Bala Rodríguez, she co-authored the poetry book *Geografías Desobedientes* (2023), featuring nude photographs of both authors taken by the photographer Patricia Águila, as they explore sexual dissidence and fat bodies. She is also the founder of FEA Editorial (Feminismo/Estrías/Autogestión), a publishing house focusing on poetic explorations of sexual and bodily dissidence.

CHILE

PABLO JOFRÉ

Oda a Querelle de Brest

El rubio narciso
humedece los labios
picotea sus besos
sobre la roca

Es Querelle
Dadá
chapero del Barrio Chino
bailando entre sus cabellos de sol
marinero en pantalones apretados
erótico mitómano gozoso.
Suicida moral

Hueles a sexo y a césped recién cortado
hipnotizas con tu ferocidad dulce e irónica.
Las miradas se multiplican en tu reflejo.
Vic deseado y asesinado.
Gil amado y traicionado.

Tu mirada de abismo
tu espalda militar
se entrega a Nono
se entrega al policía de Brest.

El tedio del bello
la fuerza del marino
tu instinto asesino.

Tu deseo es territorio
ahí respira su latencia
el amor invisible del
gato salvaje.

Todo lo purificas con la muerte.
George, Dadá.
Tus cabellos de sal
huelen a sangre y a semen.

Ode to Querelle of Brest

The blond Narcissus
wets his lips
pecks his kisses
on a rock

It's Querelle
Dada
hustler from Barrio Chino
dancing in his sunshine hair
sailor in tight trousers
erotic joyous mythomaniac.
Moral suicidal

You smell of sex and of freshly cut grass
you hypnotise with your sweetened ironic ferocity.
Glances multiply in your reflection.
Desired and murdered Vic.
Loved and betrayed Gil.

Your gaze of the abyss
your military back
he surrenders to Nono
he surrenders to the policeman of Brest.

The beau's tedium
the sailor's strength
your killer instinct.

Your desire is a terrain
there it breathes his latency
the invisible love of
the wild cat.

You purify everything with death.
George, Dada.
Your hair of salt
smells of blood and semen.

PABLO JOFRÉ

Esencia

A veces, entre tanta calle, tantos malos sueños, tanta melancolía retorcida; a veces, entre tanto sentir, tanto razonar, tanto recordar, tanto indecidirme de todo, tanto pensar en Usted (en él, en ellos) desdibujado; a veces: todas mis multitudes se detienen, se callan, despiertan de su histeria estresante y vacía. Y escucho aquel sonido irreal. La propia naturaleza, la intimidad orgánica, que se desliza por los oídos como el fluido tibio de nuestro reflejo.

Essence

Sometimes, in the midst of so many streets, so many bad dreams, so much twisted melancholy; sometimes, in the midst of so much feeling, so much reasoning, so much being undecided about everything, so much thinking of a blurred You (of him, of them), sometimes: all my multitudes stop, fall silent, wake up from their stressful and empty hysteria. And I listen to that unreal sound. Nature itself, the organic intimacy that slips through the ears like the warm fluid of our reflection.

PABLO JOFRÉ

PABLO JOFRÉ (b Chile, 1974) is a poet living and working in Berlin, Germany. Jofré was awarded the Lagar Prize by the Chilean National Contest of Literature Gabriela Mistral (La Serena) for the poetry collection *Abecedario* in 2009. He also won first prize at the Sant Andreu de la Barca Competition (in Spain) for his poem "La Danza de la Existencia (Extranjería)" in 2010.

CHILE

COLOMBIA

FLOR BÁRCENAS FERIA

El agua de los sueños

> *Rotas están las puertas de la tierra*—Czelaw Milosz

Pescar del agua del sueño una puerta abierta
que te lleva al patio de tu infancia
para decirle a tu padre que no sacrifique animales frente a ti
que no haga pactos con tu dolor
para honrar su apellido
ni que use el patio para festines con tiros al aire
mientras tu fragilidad es descubierta sola
delante de tu garganta
sólo escuchada por el río

Abrir la puerta
y detener siete veces la mano de tu padre
y siete veces perdonarle
y siete veces escribirle el mensaje en su sangre:
La infancia hala como la criatura banca
ahogada en el centro del río.

COLOMBIA

The Water of Dreams

> *Broken are the gates of Earth*—Czelaw Milosz

Fishing from the water of sleep an open door
that leads you to the patio of your childhood
to tell your father not to sacrifice animals in front of you
not to make pacts with your sorrow
to honour his surname
or use the patio for feasts with shots in the air
while your fragility is revealed alone
before your throat
only heard by the river

To open the door
and seven times to stop your father's hand
and seven times to forgive him
and seven times to write the message in his blood:
childhood pulls like the white creature
drowned in the middle of the river.

FLOR BÁRCENAS FERIA

FLOR BÁRCENAS FERIA (b Montería, Colombia, 1997) is an Afro-Caribbean poet and the author of the poetry collection *Bramidos de agua dulce* (2020). She won the young poetry Jorge García Usta prize in PoeMaRío Barranquilla. Her poetry has been included in the anthology *Como la flor: contemporary Colombian cuir poetry* edited by Planeta. Her poems circulate in national and international magazines.

COLOMBIA

ANA LÓPEZ HURTADO

Milagro

el lenguaje construye más
de lo que el cuerpo delata

el cuerpo suda
llora
y menstrúa

contrae comisuras
sonríe

digiere masas
aprieta dientes

dilata arterias y poros que
responden al tacto

saberse *ella* o *elle*
erizarse como el otro
salivar igual que el otro

sentir comezón
quemazón
o raspadura
igual que
le otre

habitarse
en la lengua
más allá
del lenguaje

saborearse cuerpa
organismo
que siente

Miracle

language builds more
than the body gives away

the body sweats
cries
and menstruates

contracts commissures
smiles

it digests masses
clenches teeth

dilates arteries and pores that
respond to touch

know oneself she or they
bristle like the other
salivate like the other

an itching
burning
or scratching
the same like
them

inhabit
the tongue
beyond
language

to savour the she-body
organism
that feels

ANA LÓPEZ HURTADO

sentarse ante el eco
de las voces que te enuncian
y reír decididamente

solo yo me nombro:
encanto que transita la piel
maraña ensueño resguardado
                                      milagro que respira

COLOMBIA

to sit before the echo
of the voices that enunciate you
and laugh decisively

only I name myself:
charm that travels through the skin
tangle, trance, sheltered

                    miracle that breathes

ANA LÓPEZ HURTADO

ANA LÓPEZ HURTADO (she/they, b 1993, Colombia) is a Colombian poet and researcher. Her first poetry book *Aquí donde tiemblo* was published in 2021 by Sincronía Casa Editorial. She is also part of *Como la flor,* an anthology of Colombian cuir (queer) contemporary poetry published by Editorial Planeta. Her poems and critical work appear in magazines such as *Río Grande Review, Círculo de poesía, La trenza, El Hipogrifo,* and *Portal Magazine* among others. Ana is currently a doctoral candidate in Latin American Studies at UT Austin. Her academic research focuses on the intersections between paid domestic work and affect in Colombia. She holds graduate and undergraduate studies in Latin American literature.

COLOMBIA

COSTA RICA

RONALD CAMPOS LÓPEZ

La simple infinitud

No. Tú no besas, Víctor.
Besan los designios
que dolerán el hombre.
Besa la culpa nuestra de cada noche.
¡De tu juego y mi juego que hou amamos!
Aquí.
Donde echamos la vida
bajo la luna,
sobre la sábana.
Aquí donde emprendimos la simple infinitud
de besar lo terrible sobre el labio.

Varón sobre mi frente laborioso,
tú no digas que yo vengo hasta ti
para subir y llamarte a la más
doble de las ausencias.
Y a abrazarte.
¡Y a mordisquear duraznos en tu voz
y a mancharme de inocencia luego hacia la noche!
Porque las piedras parecen haber
alcanzado al tiempo y, sin embargo, tú y yo apenas
nos reconciliamos con la muerte.

Por eso, acéptale sus victorias a este cielo,
amado mío,
que yo acepto tu senil mano
y, con ella,
mi postrer desolación en tu otoño.

The Simple Infinity

    No. You don't kiss, Victor.
The designs
that will hurt man kiss.
Our nightly guilt kisses.
Of your game and mine, we love each other!
Here.
Where we cast our life
under the moon,
on the bedsheets.
Here, where we began the simple infinity
of kissing all that is terrible on the lip.

Laborious man on my forehead,
do not say that I come to you
to climb up and call you to the most
double of absences.
And to embrace you.
And to nibble peaches in your voice
and to smear myself with innocence later into the night!
Because the stones seem to have
reached time, and yet you and I are only just
coming to terms with death.

Therefore, accept this sky's victories,
my beloved,
as I accept your senile hand
and, with it,
my last desolation in your autumn.

RONALD CAMPOS LÓPEZ

Velar tu desnudez

> *y yo velaré bien por ti*
> Yirmeyah 40,4

Sé que no me estás escuchando.
Dormido sobre ti mismo como todas las mañanas.
Dormido conteniendo un volcán, un quantum, los milenios.
Dormido, pero invitándome
tu boca.   Tu boca   ay, tu boca…
Si la penetro así entreabierta.
Aprovechando tu manía de desmentir la nada.
¡Aprovechando tu bífida lengua que deja
deforme un rastro de baba con cielos!
¡Aprovechando tus colmillos sin aviso, oh cabeza diamantada!
      Muerde.
¡Qué tu mandíbula la vida sigue, mi pene sigue!
      Muerde.
¡Qué tu boca venza dos veces, dos vveces venza a Dios!
      ¡Muerde!
Porque el hombre. Su boca entredormida.
¡El hombre o cascabel mordiéndose
es vastedad
donde Dios continúa todavía naciendo!
      ¡Muerde,
        oh sierpe de amor…!
Si me aprovecho de tu boca entreabierta.
Es porque tortuoso   descompuesto
¡agobiado de llamarte y llamarte!
soy   noctívago   con el aliento…
    quien necesita   que lo inventes

Si me aprovecho.
Oh crótalo mordiéndome.
Es porque soy
a quien un día le ordenaron

COSTA RICA

Looking after your nakedness

> *I will look well unto thee*
> Yirmeyah 40,4

I know you are not listening to me.
Asleep on yourself like every morning.
Asleep carrying a volcano, a quantum, the millenniums.
Asleep but inviting me
with your mouth.   Your mouth   oh, your mouth…
If I penetrate it ajar.
Taking advantage of your obsession with disproving nothingness.
Taking advantage of your forked tongue that leaves
a deformed trail of heavenly drool!
Taking advantage of your fangs without warning, oh diamantine head!
            Bite.
What with your jaw life goes on, my penis goes on!
            Bite.
May your mouth twice vanquish, twice vanquish God!
            Bite!
Because man. His mouth half-asleep.
Man or a rattlesnake biting
is vastness
where God is still being born!
            Bite,
                oh serpent of love…!
If I take advantage of your half-open mouth.
It is because it's tortuous   sickly
I'm tired of calling you and calling you!
I am
        who needs nocturnal that you invent me with your breath…

If I take advantage.
Oh rattlesnake biting me.
It is because I am
who one day was ordered

RONALD CAMPOS LÓPEZ

(¡da el reloj las 12:00!)
velar aquí al que verda-

de ra men te acompaña hacia la Noche...

Teotihuacán
Diciembre, 2018

COSTA RICA

(the clock shows 12:00!)
here to look after

the one who really accompanies you into the night...

Teotihuacán
December, 2018

RONALD CAMPOS LÓPEZ

RONALD CAMPOS LÓPEZ (b San José, Costa Rica, 1984) is a poet, academic, and researcher in contemporary Hispanic literature. Campos López has published many poetry collections, including *Deshabitado augurio* (2004), *Hormigas en el pecho* (2007), *Navaja de luciérnagas* (2010), *Varonaria* (2012), *Mendigo entre la tarde* (2013), *La invicta soledad* (2014), *Quince claridades para mi padre* (2015), and *Depravación de la Luz* (2021).

COSTA RICA

DAVID ULLOA

Christina Aguilera

Le he dado tres vueltas al paño alrededor de mi cabeza
y me he subido en dos plataformas prestadas
que no pienso devolver.

Oigo la señal de arranque:
"Christina, you nasty"
y sincronizo mis labios para pronunciar:
"Yeah".

Yo pintada y acinturada
en homenaje a la mejor amiga que he tenido.

Frente a mí niños,
mocosos disfrazados de treintones
en la fiesta de cumpleaños que tenían prohibida.

Felices nos aplauden
a ella y a mí.

Christina Aguilera

I've wrapped the cloth three times around my head
and I've climbed on two borrowed platform shoes
that I don't plan to return.

I hear the starting signal:
"Christina, you nasty"
and I synchronise my lips to utter:
"Yeah."

Me, with make-up and belted-up
in homage to the best friend I ever had.

In front of me, children,
brats dressed up as thirtysomethings
at the birthday party they were forbidden.

They happily applaud
her and me.

DAVID ULLOA

Joseph Farsh

Pasé demasiado tiempo examinando tu cara,
buscando aunque sea uno de los errores que me han dicho
tiene la mía.

Ni uno,
juego en desventaja.

Mi carta bajo la manga, pienso,
es la novedad.

Que cuando sepa tu nombre y te lo repita de vuelta será un sonido nuevo para vos.

Exotismo.

Nunca un tico ha dicho las palabras
Joseph Farsh.

Las digo yo.

La música está demasiado alta,
de mi boca lo que sale es un rumor.

Vos no preguntás por el mío,
perdés el interés,
volvés a la barra
y yo regreso a mi país.

Acá te llamás
Motherfucking Joe Fart.

COSTA RICA

Joseph Farsh

I spent too much time examining your face,
searching for even one of the mistakes that I've been told
mine has.

Not even one,
I play at a disadvantage.

My card up my sleeve, I think,
is the novelty.

That when I learn your name and repeat it back to you it'll be a new sound to you.

Exoticism.

Never has a Tico[4] said the words
Joseph Farsh.

I say them.

The music is too loud,
from my mouth, a rumour.

You don't ask for mine,
you lose interest
you go back to the club
and I return to my country.

Here, you are called
Motherfucking Joe Fart.

---

4 A native of Costa Rica. Costa Ricans are usually called ticos by themselves as well as by people of other Spanish-speaking countries.

DAVID ULLOA

Poesía gay

Si me voy a morir
ojalá sea apuñalado muy de noche
por hacer cruising en La Sabana
o de un ataque al corazón
chingo
en el sauna.

Rodeado de amigos.

Gay Poetry

If I'm going to die
I hope I get stabbed very late at night
for cruising in La Sabana
or from a fucking
heart attack
in the sauna.

Surrounded by friends.

DAVID ULLOA

DAVID ULLOA (b Costa Rica, 1989) published the short-story collection *Cartas a hombres* (2018), which was reprinted in 2020, and the collection of poems *Irme de todos los lugares* in 2024. He writes about the world of gay men and nostalgia as a universal experience.

COSTA RICA

CUBA

YORDÁN REY OLIVA

Mi isla

En poco tiempo aprendí la magia
de esperarte,
alargar el roce impaciente de mi corazón contra
su cueva.
Curvas imperfectas las del reloj...

Atrapé tu olor en hojas de yagruma,
pero me faltan tus ojos,
y los dedos de tocarme cada día a las seis.
Mi gato no sabe igual sin tus brumas,
y el té se enfría irremediablemente.
Me lanzaré al río, estoy cansado de remar.

CUBA

My Island

In a short time, I learned the magic
of waiting for you,
to extend the impatient rubbing of my heart against
its cave.
Imperfect curves of the clock…

I caught your scent in the leaves of yagruma,
but I'm missing your eyes,
and the fingers to touch me every day at six.
My cat doesn't taste the same without your mists,
and the tea gets hopelessly cold.
I'll throw myself into the river; I'm tired of rowing.

YORDÁN REY OLIVA

YORDÁN REY OLIVA (b Havana, Cuba, 1992) is a poet and novelist. He's the author of five books, including the children's book *Teresa Valdés del Pueblo de quita y pon* (Unicornio, 2016), the poetry collection *Cantar del niño nunca robado* (GEEPP EDICIONES, 2019), and the novel *Grutesco* (Capiro, 2019). Rey Oliva has won many awards, including the Premios Lorca IV Narrativa LGBTQ+ (España, 2013), and the Per(versus) Prize 2018.

CUBA

DOMINICAN REPUBLIC

JU PUELLO

Me Afroamo

Me miro en el espejo de una ciudad que consume mis sentires,
me miro con una sonrisa que no tiene dientes,
veo un cuerpo portador de tantos virus,
veo luces de casas en la que habita gente que nos odia,
a mí y a todxs los que somos parte de este cuerpo antinorma,
casas en las que también viven cuerpos no humanos.
Me miro con amor y un poco de tristeza,
decido regalarme los abrazos perdidos hace años,
me colmo de la ternura de mis ojos.
Me siento un dios más sensible que cristo,
me siento cada vez menos humano,
me uno a las aguas visitadas por Oshún y Yemayá,
me bautizo en sus ríos que me hacen dudar de clavos y cruces
como sacrificio por pecados inventados y plasmados en capillas.
Estoy adornando la ciudad que a veces finge adornarme a mí,
me he hecho un trono no por arrogancia,
sino en venganza por los dolores provocados a mi alma en estas calles.
Dejo de ser carne para consumo de bestias con nombres de hombres,
y me convierto en lo invisible,
me convierto en tiniebla que no conduce ni a infiernos ni a cielos,
pero sí a mundos de alienígenas.
Soy tan real como el polvo del Sahara que barre mi isla cada año,
estoy en el calentamiento global que a veces derrite mis sueños,
me tiro en la esquina de este apartamento porque a veces me
siento como la basura que se arroja diariamente en ese punto de la calle,
pero sé que no lo soy.
En este intento de poema que se viste de confesión, pongo mi alma,
lloro sin lágrimas visibles y recuerdo que no somos especiales,
pero que no somos de aquí.

DOMINICAN REPUBLIC

I Afro-Love Myself

I look at myself in the mirror of a city that consumes my tenderness,
I look at myself with a smile that has no teeth,
I see a body carrying so many viruses,
I see the lights of houses inhabited by people who hate us,
me and all of us who are part of this anti-normative body,
houses in which non-human bodies also live.
I look at myself with love and a little sadness,
I decide to give myself the hugs I lost years ago,
I fill myself with the tenderness of my eyes.
I feel like a god more sensitive than Christ,
I feel less and less human,
I join the waters visited by Oshún and Yemayá,
I am baptised in their rivers which make me doubt nails and crosses
as a sacrifice for sins invented and shaped in chapels.
I am embellishing the city that sometimes pretends to embellish me,
I have made myself a throne not out of arrogance,
but in revenge for the pains inflicted on my soul in these streets.
I cease to be flesh for the consumption of beasts with the names of men.
and I become invisible,
I become darkness that leads neither to hell nor to heaven,
but to alien worlds.
I am as real as the Sahara dust that sweeps my island every year,
I inhabit the global warming that sometimes melts my dreams,
I throw myself in the corner of this flat because sometimes I feel like the garbage that is dumped daily in that spot on the street,
but I know I am not.
In this attempt at a poem that dresses up as a confession, I leave my soul,
I cry without visible tears and I remember that we are not special,
that we are not from here.

JU PUELLO

JU PUELLO (b Dominican Republic, 2000) is an Afro-Dominican transmasculine writer, composer, and poet. He grew up in San Cristóbal surrounded by young artists who constructed revolution from poverty and marginality. His interest in rap, poetry, and narration was born there, and he eventually became part of the literary workshop "Mi barrio en letras". In 2017, he obtained a scholarship and began his migration to Honduras, an experience that marked his literature portraying the lives of sexual dissidents, black folk, the poor, and migrants, themes that run through his flesh and skin. He participated in the collective publication *Queer Life in the Margins* published by Edge Zones Press in Miami. He has published the independent fanzine *Las Vidas Negras Trans Importan* (Catinga Ediciones) and has written an unpublished poetry book *La última vida de un gato*, which was granted an award by Managua Furiosa (Ni). He currently resides in Honduras and is a member of the LGBTIQ+ creators collective "La Maricada", founder, and co-editor of the Digital Magazine *La Maricada*, an initiative that seeks to make literary and creative work visible from the perspective of sexual diversity.

DOMINICAN REPUBLIC

ECUADOR

TIBIEZAS DAGER

El autor

El autor no me mira.
El autor respira demasiado.
El autor se frota el esternón y recuerda esa vez que durante mal tiempo un estudiante apunto de hielo y besos le arrancó la próstata.
El autor valida expresiones, como fango burocrático y neoberraco.
El autor ante el título no como un pequeño dios sino como otra forma de replantear la victimización.
El autor ante un cuestionamiento de los que dentro de esta dinámica somos pueblo.
Se mantiene presentido y esférico.
El autor escribe desde el ayer priorizando de antemano lo ya superado.
Uff.
El autor suele ser varón.
Yo soy solo una tribulación
que ante la imposibilidad de ser pintor se postra escritor.

ECUADOR

The Author

The author doesn't look at me.
The author breathes too much.
The author rubs his sternum and remembers that time when in bad weather
a student about to freeze and kiss ripped out his prostate.
The author validates expressions like bureaucratic mud and neoburdensome.
The author with the title not of a small god but of another way of rethinking
victimisation.
The author questioned by those of us who, within this dynamic, are the pueblo.
He remains sensed and spherical.
The author writes from yesterday, prioritising beforehand what has already been overcome.
Phew.
The author is usually male.
I am only a tribulation
who, faced with the impossibility of being a painter, surrenders to being a writer.

TIBIEZAS DAGER

Hóspita

Una tierra de transexuales temerosas de Dios
es una nación huérfana.
Sometida al desplazamiento eterno.

A la condición de nómadas,
le llamarán libertad de movimiento.
Al abandono, le llamarán independencia.
Al aislamiento involuntario, le llamarán soledad.
Al narcisismo colectivo nombrarán comunidad.

Ahora, apunta a donde existo en tu historia.
En qué parte de tu registro personal se abulta mi rostro.

Yo sabía que los dedos del tiempo podían ser quebrados
así que intenté.

Si te vas a quedar a pasar la noche
guarda silencio y escúchame cicatrizar.

Hospitable

A land of God-fearing transexuals
is an orphan nation
subject to an eternal displacement.

To nomadic condition,
they will call it freedom of movement.
To abandonment, they will call it independence.
To the involuntary isolation, they will call it loneliness.
To the collective narcissism, they will call it community.

Now, point to where I exist in your story.
where in your personal registry my face is bulging.

I knew that the fingers of time could be broken,
so I tried.

If you are going to stay the night
keep quiet and listen to my wounds healing.

TIBIEZAS DAGER

TIBIEZAS DAGER (b Guayaquil, Ecuador, 1997) is a poet and visual artist. He has participated in many poetry festivals, including Arte=Orgullo, 3rd Encuentro Regional Poético de Santo Domingo, Vuelo de Mujer, and "Caída Común", a performance event that took place in La Paz, Bolivia. Tibiezas Dager completed an artistic residency called "Casa Aparte" in Cuenca, Ecuador. His work can be seen on his Instagram account @tibiezas.

ECUADOR

VICTORIA VACCARO GARCÍA

DESTRUCCIÓN DE LOS CUERPOS SUBLIMES

a las travestis y mujeres trans
que viven conmigo,
habitando en mí
con sus vidas y sus muertes.

ábrase mi cuerpo:

espejismo de dios primitivo
que no perdonó la iridiscencia.

alzamos las cabezas,
rotas,
bautizadas en sangre
y leche materna.

así vinimos al mundo:
lascivas, animales, calientes,
heridas de esplendor.

pecar fue nuestra muerte inaugurada.

silencios dieron nombres a nuestro cadáver.

desde las grietas
establecimos el abismo,
oscuro meridiano entre vida y no vida,

floreciendo hacia los márgenes
de un cuerpo glorificado.

*

henos aquí,
belleza terrible.

celebren nuestras manos
el apogeo de la noche.

*

ECUADOR

DESTRUCTION OF SUBLIME BODIES

*to transvestites and trans women
who live with me,
who live in me
with their lives and their deaths.*

open up body of mine:

a mirage of a primitive god
who didn't spare our iridescence.

we lifted our heads
broken,
baptised with blood
and breast milk.

this is how we came into the world:
lascivious, bestial, feverish,
wounded women in splendour.

to sin was our inaugurated death.

silences gave names to our corpse.

from the crevices
we created the abyss,
a dark meridian between life and no life,

blossoming towards the margins
of a glorified body.

*

here we are,
terrible beauty.

celebrate, our hands,
the night's apogee.

*

VICTORIA VACCARO GARCÍA

ábrase mi cuerpo
para el nuevo sol
que arderá:

                                                       corona perpetua.

ECUADOR

i

open up body of mine
for the new sun
that will burn:

                                                perpetual crown.

VICTORIA VACCARO GARCÍA

Sin título

Esta sangre que nunca pedí,
flujo de una diosa adolescente,
—océano que vino a hincar
la carne estrecha que yo amo—
surge, tiembla, se estremece;
acaso vieras su curso dirigirse
hacia la aciaga blancura,
acaso vieras en mi boca la palabra
cercenada por latitudes.
Si acaso existieras dentro de mí
para hacerte figura de dolor
en todos los cuerpos anónimos.

Untitled

This blood I never asked for,
flow of an adolescent goddess,
—an ocean that came to sink
the tight flesh that I love—
surges, trembles, it shudders;
perhaps you saw its course
towards the ominous whiteness,
perhaps you'd see in my mouth the word
severed by latitudes.
If perhaps you exist within me
to make you a figure of pain
in all the anonymous bodies.

VICTORIA VACCARO GARCÍA

VICTORIA VACCARO GARCÍA (b Guayaquil, Ecuador, 1998). Poet, trans woman, feminist. Her texts have been published in Despertar publishing house's blog and in magazines such as *Tangente, Pie de Página, Liberoamérica, Elipsis,* and in the *Periódico de Poesía de la UNAM*. Her first collection of poems, *Árbol ginecológico*, was published by the Minga Poética imprint of the fanzine publishing house Crímenes en Venus (Guayaquil, 2020) and by Libero Editorial (Madrid, 2021). Her second collection, *Breve mitología del cuerpo original*, won the Ana María Iza Poetry Prize for Women Writers. She is currently studying Literature at the Universidad de las Artes de Guayaquil.

ECUADOR

EL SALVADOR

ALBERTO LÓPEZ SERRANO

EL VELERO II

Me gusta contemplar mi piel desnuda
bañándose en el río, irresistible,
palparla con mi ejército invencible
de dedos que me bajan la bermuda.
Piel silenciosa y tibia, siempre aguda
mientras yo la recorro así flexible,
con cosquilleo en celo incontenible
bajo el vaivén del agua que me escuda.
Yo navego desnudo en este río
y me gozo con cada miembro mío
palpado amenamente por completo.
Del más fino cabello hasta las plantas,
yo te amo, cuerpo mío, que me encantas,
y es mi cómplice el río en el secreto.

EL SALVADOR

THE SAILING BOAT II

I enjoy contemplating my naked skin
as it bathes in the river, so irresistible,
and feeling it with my army of invincible
fingers pulling my Bermuda shorts down.
Warm and silent skin, always with such acuity
as I run through it like this, an elastic pleat,
with a tingling in an irrepressible heat
under the swaying water that shields me.
I sailed naked on this river
and I rejoice with every limb of mine,
fondly felt in its entirety.
From the finest hair to the soles,
I love you, body of mine; you enchant me,
and the river is my accomplice in this secret.

ALBERTO LÓPEZ SERRANO

ALBERTO LÓPEZ SERRANO (b El Salvador, 1983) teaches English and mathematics. He is a Member of the Alkimia Cultural Foundation and coordinator of the project Wednesday of Poetry since 2008. Alberto manages The Writer's House — Salarrué Museum of the Ministry of Culture of El Salvador. He is the Director of the International Poetry Festival "Amada Libertad" and the Poetry Festival of San Salvador, as well as being a member of the poetry collective THT. He has participated in festivals, meetings, and fairs throughout Central America, Mexico, Cuba, Peru, Bolivia, and Colombia. He has published the following poetry books: *The ship is missing* (2007), *A hundred sonnets of Alberto* (2009), *And how impossible not to call your groin* (2009), *Mountain and other poems* (2010), *The horse tamer* (2013), and *Songs for my boys* (2014).

EL SALVADOR

GUATEMALA

MANUEL GABRIEL TZOC BUCUP

FECALIDAD EN EL OLVIDO

Observando las cosas de mi baño
me pregunté por las pequeñas fecalidades que quedan en ellas
y ahí están los cuerpos futuros y cínicos
limpiándose las culpas con jabón gel sin aroma

Exacto nene
los cuerpos sin futuro
SOMOS NOSOTROS
limpiando y ensuciando el corazón con el deseo
de escribir en medio del abismo

Reconstruir el crimen de vivir el día a día
abrazando nuestro libro preferido
regando cada mañana una planta de amapolas
observando el mar infestado de petróleo
abrazando un cuerpo muerto y aún tibio
acariciando perros callejeros
en fin y por fin
esto es la fecalidad de los años felices

La crónica roja del día
llena de obligaciones domésticas y laborales
¿estamos solos o nos sentimos solos?
la verdad es singular en cada sujeto
no puedo a hablar por ti nena
lo siento
aunque me odies
yo desapareceré en cualquier momento
reconstruyendo la malvada historia de nuestras vidas

GUATEMALA

FECALITY IN OBLIVION

Looking at the things in my bathroom
I wondered about the little fecalities left in them
and there, the future and cynical bodies
wiping their guilt with unscented soap gel

Exactly baby
the bodies without future
ARE US
cleansing and dirtying the heart with the desire
to write in the midst of an abyss

Reconstructing the crime of living day by day
embracing our favourite book
watering every morning a poppy plant
watching the oil-infested sea
embracing a dead body, still warm
caressing stray dogs
at last and at last
this is the fecality of the happy years

The red chronicle of the day
full of domestic and work duties
Are we alone or do we feel alone?
the truth is singular in each subject
I can't speak for you baby
I'm sorry
even if you hate me
I'll disappear at any moment
reconstructing the malevolent story of our lives

MANUEL GABRIEL TZOC BUCUP

EXORCISMO MARIKA Y MIXTER POPPERS

He visto a la poesía fornicar delante de mis ojos
literalmente la metáfora de la orgía carnal frente a mí
participo de lamer hongos llenos de leche
de succionar con mi lengua estrellas negras llenas de placer
el grito volcánico de los sexos colectivos
el eco de los gemidos pegados en las paredes del cuarto oscuro
y mi corazón late
mi ano late
mi verga late
mi amor late por todos estos cuerpos calientes
pegados a mi carne
somos el festín sexual de huesos
penetrando huesos

GUATEMALA

MARIKA EXORCISM AND MIXTER POPPERS

I have seen poetry fornicate in front of my eyes
literally the metaphor of carnal orgy in front of me
I take part in licking mushrooms full of milk
of sucking with my tongue black stars full of pleasure
the volcanic scream of collective sexes
the echo of moans stuck on the walls of a dark room
and my heart beats
my anus beats
my cock beats
my love beats for all these hot bodies
clinging to my flesh
we are the sexual feast of bones
penetrating bones

MANUEL GABRIEL TZOC BUCUP

MANUEL GABRIEL TZOC BUCUP (b San Andrés Xecul, Totonicapán/Guatemala City, 1982) is a Mayan K'iche' poet, and visual and performance artist from Iximulew. He has published a number of books in alternative presses, and his texts have appeared in literary magazines and anthologies throughout Abya Yala. He has presented his visual art in galleries and contemporary art shows locally and internationally. Tzoc Bucup is one of the founders of Maleta Ilegal, a small, independent, handmade publishing outfit that carries out limited print runs. He spearheaded the publication of one of the first queer poetry collections in Central America, *Antología LGBTIQ+ Guatemala* (e/X, 2018).

GUATEMALA

HONDURAS

YASÓN SERRA

Origen

Se hizo, entonces,
                    el nombre
y de mis dedos la señal
el beso lo eterno
el encuentro plural
la constelación y el eclipse.

Fue dos veces la noche
y el día el pestañeo de los árboles
las bestias,
            colmillos y sangre
asesinaron su estirpe
por darnos a luz
y firmar el contrato.

Origin

In the beginning, then,
                the name
and from my fingers, the sign
the kiss the eternal
the plural encounter
the constellation and the eclipse.

It was twice the night
the day the blinking of trees
the beasts,
        fangs and blood
they murdered his lineage
for giving us birth
and signing the contract.

YASÓN SERRA

Oveja

Elígeme a mí, amado mío,
rasga mis vestidos lácteos
haz de mi cuerpo perverso
la lumbre
                del camino postrero
bésame con el sueño que no acaba
úngeme con el silencio virginal
del delito.

Aunque no merezca de vos
ya más nada.

HONDURAS

Lamb

Choose me, my beloved,
tear my milky clothes
make my perverse body
the fire
       of the last road
kiss me with the dream that does not end
anoint me with the virginal silence
of crime.

Even if I don't deserve from you
anything more.

YASÓN SERRA

YASÓN SERRA (b Tegucigalpa, Honduras, 1996) is a homoerotic artist, also known as Erático, and a university teacher and writer. Among his books are *Principio de antítesis* (2022) and *Anhedonias* (2023). His social media handles are @yasonserra / @eratic00 He recently won the literary residency 'Habitación propia' in A Coruña, Spain.

HONDURAS

V. ANDINO DÍAZ

Poetas enamoradas

Tegucigalpa sudorosa y excitada
Decime ¿qué tenés para dar esta noche a las poetas enamoradas?
Que no sea lluvia porque no tienen techo
Guardalas del peligro de tus calles solitarias
Pasean por tus caderas perdidas
Crean versos en camas bulliciosas
Se ahogan con tu afán de verlas volver a tus cadenas
Quizás mañana encuentren un refugio de tu caótico grito, de tus venas hediondas, de tu
mentira constante de una vida mejor
Árbol moribundo que pudre al fruto que carga
No dejés a las poetas dormir esta noche
Que tu desesperanza no las persiga

Female Poets in Love

Sweaty and aroused Tegucigalpa
Tell me, what do you have to give tonight to the female poets in love?
Let it not be rain because they don't have a roof over their heads
Guard them from the danger of your lonely streets
They stroll along your lost hips
They create verses in clamorous beds
They drown on your eagerness to see them return to your chains
Maybe tomorrow they'll find a refuge from your chaotic cry, your stinking veins, your constant lie of a better life
A dying tree that rots the fruit it bears
Don't let the female poets sleep tonight
Let not your despair haunt them

V. ANDINO DÍAZ

Alienígena

No soy de este mundo,
Ni de sus aceras diminutas,
Ni de las esquinas meadas,
Ni de los cerros de basura.
Soy de barro y sal;
Llevo en mi ADN agua de riachuelo,
Nacido de cuerpos podridos,
Forjado con puntas de jade.
No soy de este mundo desigual,
Falso,
De máquinas humeantes.
Soy resistencia,
Cuerpo gordo
Liberado.

Alien

I am not of this world,
nor of its tiny pavements,
nor of the pissy corners,
nor of the hills of rubbish.
I am of mud and salt;
I carry in my DNA polluted water,
Born of rotting bodies,
I'm forged with jade tips.
I am not of this unequal world,
False,
Of smoking machines.
I am resistance,
Fat body
Liberated.

V. ANDINO DÍAZ

V. ANDINO DÍAZ (b Honduras, 2000) is a writer, illustrator, and puppeteer who creates from his fat and non-binary experiences. He is a co-founder of Colective No Binaries Honduras, member of the Compañía Teatral El Tramador, and a student of literature (UNAH), film (Escuela de Cine UMP), and graphic arts (ENBA). (@gordonobinario)

HONDURAS

MEXICO

INGRID BRINGAS

Otras geografías

Amé a una mujer en otro idioma,
hice el silencio en otro idioma,
nadie reclamó nada.

Ni amor ni palabras,
la piel muerta,
decíamos la palabra universo en otro idioma.

Y nos entendíamos con el tacto, grabamos la corteza de los árboles en otro idioma
es decir, un lugar secreto para nosotras
nos cepillamos el cabello y flotábamos
por dentro éramos las mismas entendíamos el mismo lenguaje.

Other Geographies

I loved a woman in another tongue,
I made silence in another tongue,
nobody reclaimed anything.

Neither love nor words,
dead skin,
we were saying the word universe in another tongue.

And we understood each other by touch; we recorded the trees' bark in another tongue
that is, a secret place for us
we brushed our hair and were floating
inside we were the same we understood the same tongue.

INGRID BRINGAS

Actos de pertenencia

Pertenezco a una raza de mujeres
que guardan poesía en una computadora
escriben cartas de amor en una servilleta
naturaleza muerta en un mar de violetas.

Pertenezco a una raza de mujeres
de naturaleza encendida
que escriben sobre un país sin ellas.

Pertenezco a una raza de mujeres
que son todos los animales que hemos abandonado
esta tierra
ese cuerpo
pertenezco.

Acts of Belonging

I belong to a race of women
who keep poetry in a computer
write love letters on a napkin
still life in a sea of violets.

I belong to a race of women
of kindled nature
who write about a country without them.

I belong to a race of women
who are all the animals we have abandoned
this earth
that body
I belong to.

INGRID BRINGAS

CRISTO ES UNA MUJER

Una mujer trans
que bajó desnuda de una cruz,
Cristo es todas las mujeres
que corren huyendo de árboles de navidad arrancados

De hombres blancos que rezan por ella
su cuerpo es el cuerpo de todos
encerrado en una maleta vieja dentro de un Greyhound

Una mujer es Cristo
huyendo de rostros idos
de ruinas y olvido

Cristo es una mujer que grita
frente a hombres que leen la biblia
y lloriquean en navidad con villancicos de Bing Crosby

Inmaculada y anónima
una mujer trans huye
como Cristo con un par de clavos en las manos

Pidiendo la resurrección
nombrada por Eva y Lilith

Cristo es una mujer
que devora Norteamérica
esperando una reverencia de puntillas
herida en el costado.

CHRIST IS A WOMAN

A trans woman
who came down naked from a cross,
Christ is all the women
who run away from uprooted Christmas trees

Of white men who pray for her,
her body is the body of everyone
locked in an old suitcase inside a Greyhound

A woman is Christ
escaping from dazed faces
of ruins and oblivion

Christ is a howling woman
in front of men reading the Bible
and weeping at Christmas, listening to Bing Crosby carols

Immaculate and anonymous,
a trans woman runs away
like Christ with a pair of nails in her hands

Asking for the resurrection,
being named by Eve and Lilith

Christ is a woman
who devours North America
waiting for a tip-toe bow
wounded in the side.

INGRID BRINGAS

INGRID BRINGAS (b Monterrey, Mexico, 1985) is the author of *La Edad de los Salvajes* (Editorial Montea, 2015), *Jardín Botánico* (Abismos Casa editorial, 2016), and *Nostalgia de la luz* (UANL, 2016). Her poetry has been translated into English, French, and Portuguese.

MEXICO

CÉSAR CAÑEDO

Cuando me gusta un hombre a primera vista

Cuando me gusta un hombre a primera vista
es porque se parece a alguien de mi familia.

A veces veo a mi abuelo borracho entre sus cejas
o la luz apagada de mi primo.
Las pisadas del tío favorito y mis ojos detrás, sin hacer ruido.
En todos ellos,
la manzana de adán
igual a la primera manzana que se clavó en mi espalda.
Las ganas de hablar muy hombre.
El caminar superior y prominente.

Me les quedo viendo
como si con eso desatara la fantasía.
Y cuando me miran con su desprecio
me gustan más
porque así me miraba mi padre.

When I fancy a man at first sight

When I fancy a man at first sight
it's because he looks like someone from my family.

Sometimes, I see my grandfather drunk between his eyebrows
or my cousin's extinguished light.
The footsteps of my favourite uncle and, behind, my noiseless eyes.
In all of them
is the Adam's apple,
just like the first apple nailed to my back.
The desire to talk all manly.
The superior and prominent walking.

I stare at them
as if to unleash the fantasy.
And when they look at me with contempt
I want them more
because that's how my father saw me.

CÉSAR CAÑEDO

CÉSAR CAÑEDO (b Mexico, 1988) is a poet, academic, researcher, athlete, and literary critic. He holds a degree in Hispanic Language and Literature, a Master's degree in Mexican Literature, and a PhD in Literature from the Facultad de Filosofía y Letras ffyl (UNAM). He is a lecturer at the Colegio de Letras Hispánicas de la ffyl (UNAM) and directs a seminar on Lesbian and Gay Literature at the same institution. Cañedo is the author of three collections of poetry. He won the Premio Nacional de Poesía Francisco Cervantes Vidal 2017 and the Premio Bellas de Poesía Aguascalientes 2019. He is a member of House of Apocalipstick, and also teaches creative writing workshops.

MEXICO

DANIEL NIZCUB

A ella (Que también soy yo)

*Hace tiempo que las alegrías se quedan en el baúl
a resguardo del veneno de otros.
Éste es un camino lleno de pecados.
Pero llegará el final
¿Hasta entonces nos alcanzará el olvido?*

Cómo explicaré
la extinción de su voz
y sus nuevos silencios.

O que sus palabras
ahora serán sonrisas lejanas
para quien no quiera escuchar.

Cómo justificaré su muerte
cuando amanezca
desnuda sobre la cama
con un falo imaginario en la mano
y el pecho ensangrentado.

¿Para qué disculparme de su muerte
si yo también la perderé?
Yo también presenciaré su entierro,
lanzaré a su tumba las flores que sean necesarias
para que parta feliz.

Después vivirá en mi memoria,
en las cicatrices que dejará su paso por mi cuerpo,
se asomará al espejo de vez en cuando
sólo para decir adiós.

Estará feliz de despedirse una, dos,
infinitas veces.
Le permitiré hacerlo,
que parta todas las veces posibles.

MEXICO

To Her (Who is Also Me)

*It has been a while since the joys remained inside the boot
protected from the others' venom.
This is a path full of sins.
But the end will come
Will oblivion catch up with us by then?*

How will I explain
the extinction of her voice
and her new silences.

Or that her words
will now be distant smiles
for those who don't want to listen.

How will I justify her death
when daybreak finds her
naked on the bed
an imaginary phallus in her hand
and her bloodied chest.

Why should I apologise for her death
if I, too, will lose her?
I will also witness her burial,
will throw on her grave as many flowers as necessary
so she may depart happily.

Later she will live in my memory,
in the scars she will leave on my body,
she will look into the mirror from time to time
only to bid farewell.

She will be happy to say goodbye one, two,
infinite times.
I will allow her to do it,
may she depart as often as possible.

DANIEL NIZCUB

Y todos pedirán
que pronuncie palabras en su nombre;
¡pero no lo haré!

Lloraré a mi manera: a solas con ella y en paz.

MEXICO

And everyone will ask
that I utter words in her name:
But I won't do it!

I will cry my own way: alone with her and in peace.

DANIEL NIZCUB

DANIEL NIZCUB (b Mexico City, 1984) is a poet, community radio broadcaster, and communicologist. At 12, he moved with his family to the Zapotec community of Zaachila, where he began his poetic work with the spirit of his other Mixtec root of Nuñú. In 2006, during the social and teachers' movement in Oaxaca, he worked as a producer and broadcaster for community radio. Since 2010, he has worked with civil society organisations in gender, community radio, communication, and territorial defence. He is the author of *Poesía en transición* (Pez en el Árbol, 2017), considered the first collection of poems written by a trans man in Mexico.

MEXICO

NICARAGUA

MAGALY CASTILLO

Cómo ser feliz siendo de Nicaragua

Crecí conformándome con poco,
así cualquier cosa que pasará
ya estaba sobre aviso
No esperes personas para siempre
No aspires a comer todos los días
No pienses que van a cuidarte
No te lo tomes en serio
No pongas de más en eso
Me cuesta entregarme a los hechos y personas
Vivo en un pasado donde yo puedo controlar qué pude haber
dicho o de repetir una y otra vez aquella vez donde fui feliz
o me sentí viva
¿ Amé mi vida alguna vez? Creo que sí, me rompieron el corazón y
de alguna manera ya me lo esperaba
Estaba escribiendo un guión de mis tragedias
Lamento decirles que con poco se puede ser feliz pero no nos
dejan.

NICARAGUA

How to Be Happy Living in Nicaragua

I grew up making do with little,
so whatever happened
I was already warned
Don't wait for people forever
Don't aspire to eat every day
Don't think they'll take care of you
Don't take it too seriously
Don't put too much on that
I find it hard to give myself to facts and people
I live in a past where I can control what I could
have said or repeated again and again that time when I was happy
or I felt alive
Did I ever love my life? Perhaps. They broke my heart and
somehow, I was already expecting it
I was writing the script of my tragedies
I regret to say that you can be happy with little but they won't
let us.

MAGALY CASTILLO

MAGALY CASTILLO (b Nicaragua, 1996) is a Nicaraguan feminist activist and psychology graduate who works as an actress and drama instructor. She grew up in a poor area of Estelí, a city in North Nicaragua, and faced various forms of violence during her teenage years, including discrimination, exclusion, sexual harassment, and assault. In response, she chose to become an activist. In 2015, along with other young women, she founded the theatre company Las Amapolas, with the goal of providing a space for gathering, healing, critical thinking, and reflection from a feminist perspective. After moving to Spain, she joined Feministas Autoconvocadas, a group of Catalan and Nicaraguan feminist women who work to raise awareness about the violations in Nicaragua. Magaly also collaborates with Articulación de Movimientos Sociales de Nicaragua and organises with other Nicaraguans in Spain.

NICARAGUA

PARAGUAY

EDU BARRETO

Mantenimiento y reparación

Hoy tengo a dos hombres
en casa.
Uno es plomero,
el otro electricista.
La resistencia de la ducha
se quemó
(como la espera),
hizo cortocircuito
(igual que el corazón).
Tienen espaldas anchas,
brazos fornidos
(como el amante que se fue al amanecer
o el padre que nunca tuve).
Me explican milimétricamente
lo que pasó.
Miro y deseo
que así, traduzcan mi soledad.
Por momentos me angustio,
entro en pánico.
Pero se que van a mostrarme
todo lo descompuesto
que tengo.

Maintenance and Repair

Today, I have two men
at home.
One is a plumber,
the other an electrician.
The shower's resistance
burned
(like the waiting),
it shorted out
(just like the heart).
They have broad backs,
strong arms
(like the lover who left at dawn
or the father I never had).
They explain to me millimetrically
what happened.
I look and desire
that they'd translate my loneliness in this way.
At times, I get anxious,
I panic.
But I know they're going to show me
all that's broken
in me.

EDU BARRETO

EDU BARRETO (b Asunción, Paraguay, 1978) is a designer, professor, poet, and LGBT activist. In 2016, he started the project "Bien Cerca" (Well Nearby), an initiative in which he visited squares in Asunción and read poems by various authors to passers-by to promote literature and rescue public spaces. In 2018, he published his first book, *Primera Piedra (Poesía gay bajo el agua)*. His second poetry collection was *Beso negro* (2021), with illustrations by Spanish artist Blas Nusier.

PARAGUAY

PERU

FIORELLA TERRAZAS

El meme de la cifra

La muerte de mi papá es el meme
con mayor cantidad de sellos de agua
me he puesto el saco de peluche
para fingir un abrazo
soy el chiste de la tristeza
ella se burla de mí
llueve y es halloween
he concentrado mi red
me he disfrazado de maniquí
me pinté los labios
para encontrar belleza en mi rostro
mientras me abanico con 200 dólares falsos
ya tengo lista la mascarilla y las manos
todos los celulares en alerta
todas las respuestas repetidas
todo el alcohol en aerosol en vez que en forma de sangre
pinto mis labios y abro photoshop
ahora que mi papá es una estrella
plañiré con su ausencia
pero me quedo yo
y los gatos
y los animes
y south park
y legalmente rubia
y todos los videojuegos que jugabas papá
Dios bendiga a A-MIAU-RICA, a las pantuflas con garras y a Bestia Bebé.

The Number Meme

My dad's death is a meme
with the highest number of watermarks
I put on my faux fur coat
to fake an embrace
I'm the joke of sadness
she makes fun of me
it rains and it's Halloween
I've concentrated my red
I've dressed up as a mannequin
I've painted my lips
to find beauty in my face
while I fan myself with 200 fake dollars
I have the mascara and the hands ready
all mobile phones are on alert
all answers are repeated
all alcohol in aerosol rather than in blood form
I paint my lips and open Photoshop
now that my dad's a star
I'll mourn his absence
but I remain
as do the cats
and the anime
and South Park
and Legally Blonde
and all the video games you played, dad
God bless A-MEOW-RICA, the slippers with claws and the Bestia Bebé band.

FIORELLA TERRAZAS

FIORELLA TERRAZAS aka FioLoba (b Lima, Peru, 1990) is an intense genderfluid emodark-kawaii post-depressive transfeminist neurodivergent queer poet and digital communicator. Her poems have been published on various websites, magazines, and poetry blogs in several South American countries. She is one of the editors of *Plástico Revista Literaria* (revistaplastico.com) and is part of the organising committee of the ANTIFIL festival (antifil.pe). She has published the poetry chapbooks: *Dejo cabellos en los bares* (2013), *Espinoza* (2015), *Hedores* (2017), *Los tratados de la perdedora* (2017, reprinted 2020). Her poems have been adapted to different media beyond printed paper or text on screen, using platforms such as Spotify or live streaming through her Instagram account @fioloba.

PERU

PUERTO RICO

MYR OLIVARES

Despojo

Elimino las últimas letras de mi nombre
pero aún no le digo a mi madre
no quiero que piense
que me avergüenzo de ella.

No sé cómo decirle que su nombre
que es el mismo que el mío,
es un horizonte que se borra
para abrirse a otro más amplio,
donde se ve más allá
que el blanco y el negro.

PUERTO RICO

Cleanse

I erase the last letters of my name
but still don't tell my mother
I don't want her to think
she makes me ashamed.

I don't know how to say that her name,
which is mine,
is a horizon that fades
making way for another, now broader,
where one can see beyond
black and white.

MYR OLIVARES

Rompeolas

no me han preguntado
cómo transitamos
a la(s) sombra(s)

a medias
a tientas
estrujando lo poco que queda
sin resolver los minutos
en las manecillas
de los castillos que nunca existieron
porque nos lo fueron derrumbando poquito a poquito

nosotres

también

demolimos las torres.

PUERTO RICO

Breakwater

they haven't asked me
how we make our way
to shadow(s)

half-way
gropingly
ruffling what's left
without fixing the minutes
on the clock hands
of castles that never were
because they started knocking ours over grain by grain

we

nosotres[5]

also

demolish towers.

---

5 Gender-neutral form of we in Spanish

MYR OLIVARES

Anfibio

He ido tras un panal
a buscar mis trazos,
a los hormigueros
a ver si encuentro pan.

He caminado por la arena
rastreando nidos de tortuga,
trepando ramas
tras copas de paja y barro
por si avisto polluelos
o huevos quebrantados sin cría.

Por la hendidura de los arrecifes
nacidos en los trópicos,
he buceado las selvas marinas
entre fragmentos de conchas
algas salinas en la formación de oleajes
celebrando la noche.

He cruzado por bosques despoblados
volando al ras del suelo
en paracaidismo,
pero siempre aterrizo en la orilla
como todo animal anfibio.

PUERTO RICO

Amphibian

I've sought a honeycomb
in search of my traces,
gone to anthills
looking for bread.

I've walked across sands,
tracking tortoise nests,
climbing branches,
seeking cups of mud and straw,
in case I glimpse chicks
or broken eggs without brood.

Through the cleft of reefs
born in the tropics,
I've dived sea jungles
amid conch fragments,
algae saline in surf formation,
celebrating night.

I've crossed unpopulated forests
and flown low to the ground,
in a parachute,
but I always land on the shore,
like every amphibious animal.

translated by Roque Raquel Salas Rivera

MYR OLIVARES

MYR OLIVARES (they/elle, she/ella, b Puerto Rico/Dominican Republic, 1993) is a Caribbean-Puerto Rican-Dominican writer, artist, and educator. They graduated in Journalism and Foreign Languages from the University of Puerto Rico, with studies in Theater and Women's and Gender Studies. Their poems have appeared in anthologies, among them *La Piel del Arrecife*, the first anthology of Puerto Rican trans poetry, and have been translated into several languages, including Italian, English, and Portuguese. Their focus is on Latinx, LGBTQIA+ communities, and youth, promoting social justice and inclusion. They currently reside in Houston.

PUERTO RICO

ALEJANDRA ROSA MORALES

poema [póst] umo

cuando la tarde nos regaló naranjas,
sembrar siempre fue amasar
melocotones, mangó

nunca discutimos
no nos atrevimos,
o no quisimos

las tensiones más cis-géneras
las barrimos con tierra

agarraba la pala
y tarareaba

Alex, te saqué dos hijitos
de orégano, que en el frío
se pudre, orégano, que sin ella,
no me sabe, orégano,
que ya no siembro

pero pienso, sentada,
sentade en Mayaguez,
veo abuelas pasar,
y pienso,
una vez fui una nieta feliz,
una vez

aquí, una vez aquí
desayunó ella
antes de la siembra,
entendió el calor,
con un quesito en mano,
donas o un jamónquesoyhuevo

no fue dulcera,
lo más empalagoso,

[Post]humous Poem

when evening gifted us oranges,
sowing was always kneading
peaches, mangos

we never argued,
we didn't dare,
or we didn't want to

the most cis-gendered tensions
we swept them with soil

I grabbed the shovel
and hummed

Alex, I took from you two cuttings
of oregano, which, in the cold
rots away, oregano, which without her,
I don't taste, oregano,
that I no longer sow

but she thinks sitting,
they sit in Mayaguez,
I see grandmothers passing by,
and think,
once, I was a happy granddaughter,
once

here, once here
she had breakfast
before the sowing,
she understood the heat,
with a little cheese in her hand,
donuts or hamcheeseandegg

she didn't have a sweet tooth,
the most cloying thing,

ALEJANDRA ROSA MORALES

las rosas que le sembró
a la orilla de su ventana
para que viera flores,
su encierro,
siempre fue cuido.

las únicas semillas que me importan,
germinan, si pienso,
y me mimas

mangó picadito,
uvas sin las pepas,
toronjas con azúcar
y el coco, partido,

en esta nieve lavanda,
no tengo más finca,
que la memoria de tus manos,
amasando tierra conmigo.

el banco de madera
de tu patio, hoy seco
tiene el peso,
de cada mentira
que me hice país

me enseñaste sanar,
dolores que nunca te conté.

razones que no di,
preguntas que no hice
tus cassettes sin escuchar,
alcapurrias de carne,
que nos faltó comer,
recetas, que no quiero
todavía aprender.

PUERTO RICO

the roses she sowed to her
on the shore of her window
to see flowers,
her confinement,
was always careful

the only seeds I care about,
germinate if I think of you,
and so spoil me

diced mango,
seedless grapes,
grapefruits with sugar,
and the coconut, split,

in this lavender snow
I have no more land
than the memory of your hands
kneading soil with me.

the wooden bench
on your patio, now dry,
has the weight
of each lie
that I became a country

you taught me to heal
pains I never told you about.

reasons I didn't give,
questions I didn't ask,
your cassettes I didn't listen to,
meat alcapurrias
that we missed eating,
recipes I don't want to
learn yet.

ALEJANDRA ROSA MORALES

ese tiempo, sí pasó,
ya no está,
mis manos tienen rastros,
pero ya no soy nieta,
y los domingos, ya
no siembro.

PUERTO RICO

that time did pass,
it is no more,
my hands have traces,
but I'm no longer a granddaughter,
and on Sundays,
I no longer sow.

ALEJANDRA ROSA MORALES

ALEJANDRA ROSA MORALES, AL, ALÉ (they/them, she/hers, b Santurce, San Juan, Puerto Rico, 1993) is an Afro Puerto Rican non binary writer, performer, and visual artist. They embody portals of Afro-queer liberation. Their writing has been published by the *New York Times*, *Time Magazine*, *Revista Étnica*, *80grados*, *Todas PR*.

PUERTO RICO

URUGUAY

IVIX PEREIRA

Sin título

> *(...) y moría de reminiscencias por las cosas*
> *que ya no conoceríamos y eran tan violentas e inolvidables*
> *como las pocas cosas que habíamos conocido.*
>
> "Reminiscencias"
> poema de Cristina Peri Rossi

Cuando era niña, mis Barbies hacían el amor como en las películas.
Se tapaban con una sábana, dando vueltas en la cama, besándose, una arriba de la otra, susurrando cuánto se amaban.

Por un momento imaginate la vida ideal:
vos y yo, en nuestra casa del barrio Peñarol, con una parra hermosa, debajo dos sillas blancas con posabrazos, una mesita, un repasador barato.
Una docena de gatos.
Tomando mate, escuchando la radio.
Todas viejitas y arrugadas, con sonrisas cortando nuestros rostros.

Siempre fui una idealista, que se planteaba envejecer en un contexto de ternura y amor.
Mirarte enamorada, como piano de infancia, llorar lágrimas de cocodrilo.

Y al final, morir a tu lado, acostadas en la cama, juntas, boca arriba, como Susana San Juan.

URUGUAY

Untitled

> *(...) and I died reminiscing about the things that we wouldn't know and they were so violent and unforgettable like the few things that we've already known.*
>
> "Reminiscences"
> Cristina Peri Rossi

When I was a girl my Barbies made love like in the films.
They covered themselves with a sheet, tossing and turning in bed, kissing, one on top of the other, whispering how much they loved each other.

For a moment, I imagined the ideal life:
you and I in our house in the Peñarol neighbourhood, with a beautiful vine and beneath it, two white chairs with armrests, a small table, and a cheap kitchen towel.
A dozen cats.
Us drinking mate, listening to the radio.
Us, all old and wrinkled, with smiles cutting our faces.

I was always an idealist who considered growing old in a context of tenderness and love.
To look at you in love, like a childhood piano, crying crocodile tears.

And in the end, to die next to you, lying in bed together, face up, like Susana San Juan.

IVIX PEREIRA

Sin título

Anillo de oro blanco y zafiros de miles de dólares.
Nada es suficiente, cuando sabes que ella se merece lo mejor de lo mejor.

Flor del amor de mi infancia, las locas que me han tocado,
la chica que se parecía al Chili Fernández y me hacía cosquillas que se sentían raras.
Por primera vez.

Una flor basada en traumas y atracciones problemáticas, en cólicos menstruales,
tíos muertos y cachetadas de bullys.
Era todo así de intenso, así de inmenso,
pasa que en el ambiente del baile hay mucha exigencia,
disciplina, discriminación,
pero vos fuiste la única que me miró, cuando mis ojos estaban tristes de violencia,
me llevaste al baño, pasaste cerrojo y dijiste:
"de acá no salís hasta que me digas qué te pasa".
"Qué te pasa", me dijo.
Nunca nadie antes me miró y me preguntó "qué te pasa"
Y quizás tampoco nadie me había mirado a los ojos antes.
No así.

No éramos amigas. No éramos nada, compañeras lejanas.
Y desde ese día y durante varios años, fuiste todo. Justificación infantil de mi amor
por todos los seres, por la belleza innata de las personas, por el arte de un rostro
hinchado de llanto.

Como una margarita naciendo de la corteza de un árbol.

URUGUAY

Untitled

White gold and sapphire ring worth thousands of dollars.
Nothing is enough when you know that she deserves the best of the best.

Flower of my childhood love, the crazy women I had,
the girl that looked like Chili Fernández and tickled me in a strange way.
For the first time.

A flower out of traumas and troubled attractions, in menstrual colics, dead uncles and slaps by bullies.

Everything was that intense, that immense,
the thing is, on the dancefloor, there is much demand,
discipline and discrimination,
but you were the only one who looked at me when my eyes were sad of violence,
you took me to the toilets, locked the door and said:
"You're not getting out of here until you tell me what's wrong with you.
What is wrong with you?" she said.
Never before has someone looked at me and asked me: "What's wrong with you?"
And maybe nobody had looked at my eyes before.
Not like that.

We weren't friends. We were nothing, distant classmates.
And from that day on, for several years, you were everything. A childhood excuse for my love for all beings, for the inner beauty of humans, for the art of a face swollen by crying.

Like a daisy emerging from the bark of a tree.

IVIX PEREIRA

IVIX PEREIRA (b Uruguay, 1995) is a poet and a member of the Montevideo Reading Club since 2014. In 2017, she won a mention in the Pablo Neruda competition for young poets (IMSJ, Fundación Pablo Neruda de Chile). She has participated in the Montevideo Slam and Las Piedras Slam since 2016, winning the First Prize several times. She has led poetry workshops and has given performances and readings as part of the collective En el camino de los perros. She has been a member of its editorial team since 2019.

URUGUAY

VENEZUELA

ENZA GARCÍA ARREAZA

Sin título

I'm gonna set myself on fire
to see if that is a boundary enough
I'm gonna call home
like E.T.
and I might actually disappear
and only return as a curse.

Traducción:
Detesto a mi suegra.

***

Es urgente guardar un secreto
levantar una ciudad prohibida
y prometerla a un solo habitante.
Es como volver a creer
en la consagración de los bosques
o en la mano que ensarta una Ariadna
en tu aleación de baja penumbra.
Es bueno tener un secreto
saber que hay un planeta en busca de su nombre.

***

Me pregunto si piensas lo mismo que yo
cuando hablamos
si imaginas qué hubiera sido
a tiempo
salir de las mismas clases o enemigos en común
de haber visto las mismas películas
y besarnos
como se besa la gente a los veinte años
como si los perros se pusieran de acuerdo
con las resonancias
y los libros que llegan a salvarnos
salvarnos confundidos en el eco

VENEZUELA

Untitled

I'm gonna set myself on fire
to see if that is a boundary enough
I'm gonna call home
like E.T.
and I might actually disappear
and only return as a curse.

Translation:
I hate my mother-in-law.

***

It's urgent to keep a secret
to build a forbidden city
to promise it to a single inhabitant.
It's like believing again
in the consecration of woods
or in the hand that pierces an Ariadne
in your low penumbra alloy.
It's good to have a secret
to know that there's a planet in search of its name.

***

I wonder if you think the same as I do
when we talk
if you imagine what it would have been
long ago to abandon the same classes or common enemies
to have seen the same films
and have kissed
like people kiss in their twenties
as if dogs were in agreement
with the resonance
and books that come to save us
to save us, confused in the echo

ENZA GARCÍA ARREAZA

darle razón al cuerpo urgido y no celeste
como yo ahogaría peticiones en tu boca
sí, tragar, tragar y pedir que no te guardes nada
dejar las cosas en manos
de las canciones que son el único dios relevante.

Yo no suelo ser así en mis poemas
siempre oculto algo y me doy importancia
hablo de animales antiguos y de maniobras

ahora sólo te pido que existas
que me dejes
una nota de voz riéndote
porque sabes que nunca nos veremos

excepto en lo que escribimos.

***

Me avergüenza revelar
que en el tanteo busco estrellas
supongo que ser libre es no incurrir
en la censura de los presagios
por eso te hablo a esta hora
alumbrada por un rocío siniestro
porque quiero ver todo allá arriba
pero siempre despierto en una zanja.

***

El chupacabras nunca llegó
pero yo me fui
el desierto se apuraba opuesto a un cielo coloso
y lo más duro
fue aprender a usar monedas otra vez

mentira

to agree with the body, urged and not celestial
like I'd drown petitions in your mouth
yes, to swallow, to swallow and ask that you hold nothing back
to leave things in the hands
of songs, which are the only relevant god.

I'm not like this in my poems
I always hide something and I give myself importance
I talk of old animals and manoeuvrings

now I only ask you to exist
to leave me
a voice message laughing
because you know we'll never see each other

except in what we write.

***

I'm ashamed to reveal
that in the groping I look for stars
I suppose that being free is not to incur
the censorship of omens
that's why I speak to you at this hour
lit by a sinister dew
because I want to see everything up there
but I always wake up in a ditch.

***

The chupacabras never arrived
but I left
the desert harried up opposite a colossal sky
and the hardest thing
was to learn how to use coins again
a lie

ENZA GARCÍA ARREAZA

lo más duro fue no borrarme los raspones
de las rodillas
y que las migajas que dejé para regresar
no se las comiera
el perro sin cabeza que nos rige
como signo zodiacal de mierda y opresión

ay en fin
yo me fui, compré un iPhone
la abuela murió
y puede ser
que sus plantas guarden un secreto.

VENEZUELA

the hardest thing was not to erase the scratches
from the knees
and that the crumbs I left for my return
were not eaten
by the headless dog that rules us
like a zodiac sign of bullshit and oppression

alas, in the end
I left, I bought an iPhone
grandmother died
and it may be
that her plants hold a secret.

ENZA GARCÍA ARREAZA

ENZA GARCÍA ARREAZA (b Venezuela, 1987) is a short-fiction writer, poet, and visual artist, author of *Cállate poco a poco* (2008), *El bosque de los abedules* (2010), *Plegarias para un zorro* (2012), *El animal intacto* (2015), and *Cosmonauta* (2020). In 2017 she was a resident at the University of Iowa's International Writing Program and at the Pittsburgh City of Asylum. During 2018 and 2020, she was a Fellow at the International Writers Project for endangered writers at Brown University.